How To Harness

Your

Intuitive Nature

Blanca Beyar

DEDICATION

This book is dedicated to all the light-workers, Seers and Ancient Ones in the Universe; to all the star-seeds and light bearers from the many dimensions that exist, who have come collectively to assist Earth. Thank you!

CONTENTS

Chapter 1

Defining the Intuitive Empath

There are several terms that are often used to define an Intuitive: Psychic, Empath, Clairsentient or a Seer. Although these labels can be used interchangeably to define an Intuitive, there is a distinctive characteristic that separates the Intuitive from the Psychic or Seer; the Intuitive (Empath) primarily operates on sense of "feelings" when tapping into the field of insight.

We are all emotional beings, capable of feeling each other's energies and also of discerning when someone is feeling sad or happy. However, an Empath possesses a heightened sensitivity that is capable of surpassing the ability to merely determine the emotional disposition of someone. An Empath can truly feel the emotions of others and may assimilate the feelings of others not only in their own emotional bodies, but also in their physical and mental bodies. This is why some Empaths are called Sponges; because they can literally absorb the emotions of others by merely being in their presence.

There are certain characteristics that are unique of an Intuitive Empath:

• An Empath is great listener and people are drawn to talk to them

• An Empath is either very sociable or tends to be isolated

• An Empath is generally very emotional and often cry or laugh every easily

• An Empath tends to possess a great affinity to nature, to children and to animals

• An Empath is usually attracted to the arts, music, painting, writing and are great humanitarians

• An Empath is usually a vivid dreamer or displays the ability to "see" situations before they happen

The Intuitive Empath is a natural listener who seems to always be available for others and who displays a great compassion for the emotions for others. Because of these attributes, people are usually drawn to share their lives and problems with an Empath. People usually say they feel good just by sharing their lives with an Empath or by merely being in their presence and they walk away feeling lighter and calmer. Because of this, most Empaths may find themselves attracting people like bees. People may often extend invitations to attend social gatherings because they are aware of an empath's magnetic energy and feel that they can be a spark in the crowd. Ironically, the opposite may also apply. Some Empaths are so acutely aware of their sensitivity around people that they may shy away from social gatherings and events and only interact with close friends.

Empaths are usually drawn to spend time in the purity and silence of nature because it delivers a balancing and replenishing energy to the ever-giving Empath. The natural elements within nature such as the pure vibration of trees and the calming effects of bodies of water can be very soothing. It can be said that nature is a healing sanctuary for everyone but truly can be a nourishing source for the Empath. The pure energy of children and animals—their natural ability to express unconditional love and their innocent disposition can also be an immense healing source for Empaths.

Because Empathy derives from the core of our soul's deepest expression for love and passion, its nature can be compared to the attributes similar to those who are in the creative arts. Just like artists who need to have a venue by which to express their creativity, an Empath desires to unleash all of the energy that he or she experiences and also yearns to share it with others. In many ways, Intuitive Empathy can be considered a creative art because the energy source that is experienced is as unique as the individual! For some artists, the release of creative expression may come through the composition of a song, or the magnificent creation of a painting, and for the Empath, it comes in the artistic form of being able to translate energy waves into words and messages. Empaths naturally tap into their creative channel whenever they are "reading" an individual and much like a painter, sitting in front of an empty canvas, he or she awaits for the inspiration to rise from the creative field to begin to edge the foundation for what will hold a greater potential. So, too, does the Empath draw for his or her creative energies to "paint images of what she or he sees and feels to the receiver of messages.

Dreams are often another state of consciousness that we tap into while the physical body rests. I use the word "often" as opposed to "always" because some dreams are constructed from real life experiences and emotions that are felt during our wakeful state and then expressed through our dreams. However, for those who are intuitive, dreams may often be an interpretation of a vision that has a real potential outcome in the future.

Here, again, I emphasize on the word "potential." It is important to remember that as Empaths or Seers, we are able to tap into the tapestry of a potential seed of intention or outcome that may or may not take fruition. The reason for this is that as creators, individuals are constantly creating and recreating their future seeds of potential. The creation matrix is always changing and shifting as we execute the countless thoughts, words and actions in our lives. For this reason, as Empath, I always invite receivers of messages to understand that anything that I share is only a potential. I invite them to explore the potential seeds of intentions and tell them that if it resonates, then, they should fuel and feed the intention with energy. If, however, a message does not resonate, then, it is possible for them to re-shift the potential of a particular seed that is in motion by redirecting their energy to another potential outcome.

Of course, as powerful as we are as creators, there are certain outcomes that we cannot tamper with. This is not because we are not co-creators, but more so because there are certain events that need to occur for the highest outcome that has been orchestrated by the higher Source. In other instances, certain events may need to manifest for the completion of another's soul contract, in which case, no one can interfere with that soul's purpose and spiritual journey.

Empathy and Feelings

Feelings are the primary sensory that Empath utilize in connecting with others. This explains why some Empaths may experience a host of emotions, all at once, especially when they are in a group setting. It also explains why some Empaths tend to go into isolation rather than being subjected to settings where there will be large numbers of people. An Intuitive Empath is much like an antenna; a channel that can tap into more than one reception or frequency at the same time. Sometimes, much like a radio station that is coming in with static because it is not tuned in to the proper channel, an Empath can experience a static feeling of mixed emotions because she or he is picking up more than one frequency. Oftentimes, these feelings of scattered energies are signals that an Empath needs to learn how to ground and to harness themselves in order to be a clearer channel for the surrounding energies. Without the ability to ground, Empaths may be subjected to experiencing imbalances in the reception of energies which can often perpetuate feelings of anxiety, of overwhelmeness and emotional instability. Poor grounding can also interfere in the delivery of clear messages to others. In Chapter 5, we will learn more about how to ground and how to strengthen your empathic energy.

In truth, an Empath does not have to be compromised by surrounding energies in order to experience and fulfill his or her mission to be a vehicle of healing for others. In learning how to identify the characteristics of Empathy, an individual who is born with this beautiful calling can begin to learn how to harness and honor the feelings they are experiencing and recognize them more as "tools" for the art instead of a feeling of nuisance.

A balanced Empath is blessed with the attributes of unconditional love, of compassion and also lovingly detachment. The ability to love unconditionally allows an Empath to move beyond the feelings of judgments of any given disposition that someone may be displaying and to recognize that any feelings of emotional disharmony are merely being held because there is an absence of unconditional love. An absence of love is usually the root cause of many ill feelings. When we are able to move into a state of compassion, we are in a better position to offer loving insight and helpful guidance that can assist someone to heal or to introduce them to solutions that will help them achieve some kind of resolution to their conflicts.

The principle of lovingly detachment is essential to Empathic work. *Lovingly Detachment* illustrates that we should love and support others without allowing ourselves to become emotionally attached to their feelings, nor to the choices they make or to any projected outcome. By practicing lovingly detachment, we honor the journey of

13

each soul, recognizing that their choices are powerful steps in their spiritual growth. As Empaths, we can surely offer our insight and introduce an invitation for others to explore the potential of any insight that is given, however, we stay away from having expectations or refrain from taking it personal if someone does not adhere to following the insight given.

Now that you have become familiar with the traits and characteristics of an Empath, it is time to take a quiz to discover the level of your Empathic energy. Answer each question as authentically as you can by responding Yes or No to each question.

Quiz

1. Do you feel the emotions of others?
2. Do you feel impacted by the emotions of others?
3. Do you consider yourself to be a "sponge;" a person who absorbs the energies of others?
4. Are people drawn to talk to you and share their problems?
5. Do you feel like you need to counsel others; give them advice?
6. Are your emotions impacted whenever you are in large group settings?
7. Do you prefer being in quiet places?
8. Do you cry easily when speaking to people or watching movies?
9. Do you have a deep connection with nature?
10. Are you drawn to children?
11. Do you like pets and animals?
12. Do you often get guts feelings or premonitions about events or situations?
13. Do you dream often?

14. Have your dreams manifested into reality?
15. Do you have a passion to be of divine service?
16. Do you feel that your calling is to help people?
17. Are you drawn to spiritual topics or venues?
18. Do you remember having empathic experiences as a child?

Scoring Tally up your Yes and No responses.

1-6 Yes responses indicate that you are tapping into the "normal" range of empathic energy that most people generally tap in to.

7-13 Yes responses indicate that you are tapping into your empathic energy above normal range and that it may be part of your soul's calling to further develop your empathic energies in order to help others with your skills.

14-18 Yes responses indicate that you are a natural Empath and that you are tapping into a higher realm of frequency that can allow you to harness and share your gifts with others!

Exercise:

In a journal or notebook, begin to write a letter to "Yourself." In your letter, share your impressions and feelings about what you have read and learned in this chapter. As you capture your impressions, invite yourself to expand your consciousness and to explore and welcome any early memories in your childhood that may have presented the presence of your empathic abilities.

Your letter can be as lengthy as it need be, as long as you are feeling a flow of exploration and rediscovery as you write it. Have fun and feel free to discuss your true feelings of empathy. When you are done, read the letter to yourself and notice how you feel. Do you feel excited? Happy? Experience the new feelings of discovery.

Chapter 2

The Five Senses and Intuition

In chapter 1, we learned that Empaths are primarily "feelers." In chapter 2, we will explore the five senses and learn how an Empath utilizes the senses in order to feel and interpret empathic messages. First, let us begin by defining feelings:

"Feelings can be experienced by a sense of touch, experienced emotionally through a perception, feelings can be a particular impression sensed through appearance, and also through instinctive awareness."

An Empath is synonymous in many ways to the term "Clairsentient." A Clairsentient is someone who experiences "gut feelings" that can literally be felt in the physical body and may often manifest as an abdominal feeling of nervousness, of butterflies or anxiety. For some, the sensations of the "feeling" may be felt in other parts of the body such as rapid heartbeats or a tingling sensation in the head. Although these sensations may sound uncomfortable and unpleasant, they are not intended to cause discomfort. Rather, the feelings that an Empath or Clairsentient feel are signals that they are tapping into another field of energy other than their own.

As we can see, feelings can be interpreted through the five senses and conversely, the five senses can be utilized to express feelings. An Empath can use his or her five senses to assimilate the messages that are being felt through an energy connection. There is no exact protocol or rule of thumb for empathic work. We are all unique and as such, some of us may utilize one or more of our senses in order to assist us in conveying the messages that we are feeling. Let us explore the five senses and learn some of the many ways an Empath can use them as a tool.

The Five Senses and Empathic Work:

Sight:

An Empath can use her sense of vision to connect to an individual. Some Empaths can see colors or auras around people and use the colors schemes that are present to interpret a person's current state of emotional, physical and mental well-being. It is beneficial to remember that each color could literally represent a unique emotion to an Empath. For example, the color red can represent feelings of anger to one Empath and a feeling of passion to another. What is important to remember is that an Empath is tapping into a field of "feelings" and then using the sight of color to express them. .

Some Empath may not see auras or colors around an individual but may simply need to look into the person's eyes and be able to "feel" the emotions that the person is experiencing. As an Empath, I am able to use photographs to connect to individuals. I can feel the immediate energy around them and also tap into their feelings, fears, goals, etc. by simply looking at the photo and using my sense of feelings to tap into the energy field.

Hearing:

The sense of hearing is associated with Clairaudience. For the Empath or clairaudient, hearing does not necessarily mean "hearing with the ears" or audio frequency—although this sense can develop in that way. Rather, hearing is experienced as an inner-frequency; a subtle voice that most people hear...it is called intuition.

Everyone, whether they are aware of it or not, can "hear" that still voice within that often speaks to us when we are contemplating a situation, looking to make a decision or when we are simply tuning in to our spirit through meditation. The Clairaudient Empath can tap into the sense of hearing on a much higher frequency than most people. She or he is usually very sensitive to loud noises or large crowds because the sensitivity to sounds may be magnified 100 fold in the form of energy.

Taste:

In my observation, Taste is the least common sensory that an Empath utilizes in the development of Empathy. However, for those who do use the sense of taste, it can be a very powerful way to deliver messages—especially regarding the biology of the body. Although it MUST be emphasized that Empathic work does not nor should not engage in making any kind of medical diagnosis, the Empath who uses taste as a primarily sensory may very possibly detect imbalances in the body such as sugar levels, acidity, etc. They may also be able to detect any medications or substances and/or may be able to taste any deficiencies in the energy of someone. For this reason, an Empath who primarily utilizes the sensory of taste may benefit in pursuing a career in holistic nutrition or naturopathy and use their empathic abilities to complement their holistic vocation.

Smell:

The sense of smell, just like taste, is one of the lesser common sensory that an Empath usually harnesses. There is no rhyme or reason for this observation; there is no right or wrong way for an Empath to use his or her sense of sensory. The Empath will use whatever senses she or he is most sensitive to or a combination of the senses simply because this is their dynamic makeup.

In my professional observation, though, the sense of smell is most commonly used when an Empath is also gifted with the ability of Medium-ship. The ability to be a medium opens up the sensory to be able to sense and communicate with the afterlife. Again, some individuals are naturally born to be an Empath or a Medium but oftentimes, the possession of a heightened sense of energies can open the door for other hats within the holistic/spiritual arena to develop.

An Empath/Medium may use the sense of smell to communicate with the afterlife and detect a familiar scent; a perfume or cologne that was uniquely associated to a beloved passed one. A common scent is that is often experienced by an Empath are the smell of flowers but this is not exclusive to an Empath, as many family members experience the scent of flowers after the loss of a loved one. The sense of smell is not limited to perfume or flowers but can also be associated to a favorite food; the smell of freshly baked bread or cookies, or a particular dish that intoxicated the kitchen with aroma and that the beloved passed one often commented about when he or she was alive. Truly, the possibilities are limitless when an Empath has harnessed his or her five senses and utilize them to translate messages!

Touch:

The sense of touch is probably the most used by Empaths besides the sense of sight. There is something very intimate and special when the sense of touched in incorporated in reading energy. The action of touch can be performed in a variety of ways for an Empath. It could simply be to hold someone's hand and connecting to their emotional field. Giving someone a hug can also be a very effective way to not only read their energy but to also offering love and healing— energies that come natural to a Empath! For others, it is the ability to hold an object in their hands; perhaps something that is worn or used by an individual. For an Empath/Medium, the sense of touch can be very useful to connect to a beloved passed one in the Afterlife.

The Beauty of the Five Senses

We were gifted with five amazing senses that allow us to experience life. In them, we can indulge in the great feelings of capturing beauty, both in sight and sound. We are also adorned with the delicious senses to taste and to smell the infinite flavors of foods and all the beauty that is around us to partake in. And our sense of touch allows us to not only express and render affection to those that we love; we are also capable of operating and managing a unimaginable amount of tasks simply through the sense of touch!

The Empath is gifted with an enhanced ability to utilize his or her senses to levels that can go way beyond the physical experience and incorporate this heightened sensitivity to connect to others on a deep emotional and spiritual level. What is important is to remember that there should be no comparison or sense of inadequacy if other Empaths are able to develop and harness more than one of the five senses to connect to energy. Being multi-dimensional is a wonderful thing but it is also beautiful to possess a specialty in one of these attributes.

If you recognize that you possess a sensitivity to one of the five senses, allow yourself to fully develop it and devote yourself to enhancing it to the best of your ability. In time, if it is meant for you to develop any other sensory, you will be intuitively guided to notice that your scope of empathic perception is increasing and expanding. You may notice that you are tapping into the areas of "feeling" and just your awareness alone will begin to trigger your inner-development to a new height. I hope you have enjoyed learning about the five senses and I encourage you to keep this lesson handy as you continue with this course and your development.

Exercise

Materials needed: a notebook and pen

For this exercise you are invited to partner up with a volunteer that can sit with you as you begin to work on harnessing your five senses. If you cannot partner up with someone, or rather not, I will offer an alternative method to complete this exercise.

Sit comfortable in front of your partner. Ask him or her to envision a strong feeling about something; it can be something like sitting in front of a calming pond and hearing the birds singing or it can be eagerly riding on a rollercoaster. Tell your partner to use his or her feelings to create the image in their mind and also tell them not to share it with you.

As you begin to connect to your partner's feelings, notice which sensory you are tapping into in order to experience his or her feelings. Take notice of anything that you see, hear, smell or taste. Focus on your own feelings as you attempt to connect to your partner's vision.

Take your notebook and write down any impressions that you receive and also highlight how you received the information. Which sensory did you utilize to get the insights that you received? Spend about 10 minutes if you can, connecting to your partner's feelings. Take time to use your sense of sight to look at your partner; look at his or her eyes to see if you get any impressions. Also look above his or her head; do you see any colors? If you do, how does the color make you feel?

When the 10 minutes are up, turn to a clean page in your notebook and ask your partner to write a small paragraph about what they were envisioning. Ask them to be detailed in every aspect of what they were envisioning; the action, the surroundings, any colors or objects that were incorporated in the vision, etc. Compare notes and see if you were able to tap into your partner's vision. Were you able to capture the action, the feeling or able to smell or taste anything?

Please do not be discouraged if you were not able to tap into your partner's vision. Remember that your Empath abilities are like a muscle; it needs to be worked on in order for it to get strong! Feel free to practice this exercise as often as you like, making sure that you take notes of any impressions that you feel as you practice and also paying close attention to your feelings and your five senses.

Variation to this Exercise without a Partner

Call a friend or family member and ask them if they can spend ten minutes on the phone with you to help you with this exercise. Invite them to create a vision in their minds and to bring as much feelings into their vision as possible. Sit with your notebook and try to connect to their vision by bringing your attention to your feelings and senses. Take copious notes of your impressions. When you feel ready, ask your friend or family member to share their vision with you. Take note of any similarities. This exercise can be practiced as many times as you like.

Note: It is important to ask your friend or family member to share their experiences with you before you share your impressions with them.

Meditation: Activating your Five Senses

For this mindful meditation, you will need about 30 minutes of quiet time. Begin by taking a comfortable sitting position and taking a gentle but full inhale through your nostrils, and then exhaling through the mouth. Wait a few moments and then repeat a inhale and exhale breathe. Notice that you are feeling calmer and more in touch with your inner-self. At the end of your second exhale, bring your inner-attention to your third-eye, the area between your two physical eyebrows. This is the spiritual eye, the single eye; the eye of your empathic and intuitive nature. Get acquainted with this sense and as you do, notice if you are experiencing any heightened awareness in your five senses.

If you do, try to connect deeper to that sense; to seeing, hearing, smelling, tasting or feeling with your inner-eye. Explore gently, with no expectations or hesitancy. Just explore. Just feel. When you are ready to return to your body, thank your spirit for guiding you through this mediation and promise to return often.

Chapter 3

The Sixth Sense; the Empath (Intuitive) Channel

As we begin chapter 3, I will be referring to the Empath as a "Vessel." A vessel is a portal or a bridge, if you may, by which energy is channeled and transmitted.

Although we have learned that an Empath primarily uses the sense of "feelings" to receive and transmit messages, there is also a central "portal" that immensely helps an Empath to develop the skill of empathy: It is the sixth sense, the Empath's Channel.

In order to fully comprehend what the sixth sense is we will need to dedicate some time to briefly discuss the Chakras system of the Spiritual body. The Chakras system is composed of seven primary vortexes—or portals, if you may, that are present in the spiritual/energetic field of the body. The Chakras are not literally part of the physical body, but rather, the "organs of the spiritual body."

Each of the primary seven Chakras has a location in the energetic body, aligned perfectly within the spinal area. Each chakra also has a very unique characteristic of energetic input and output. Finally, each chakra is associated with a distinct aspect of the physical and spiritual bodies that monitors both the physical energy and the spiritual evolution of the soul.

The sixth chakra is known as the "third-eye or Single eye." The third-eye chakra is directly associated with divine perception, divine vision and divine knowingness. This chakra is known as the single eye because it represents the divine vision of the One Source that is within all of us. It is from this chakra that we can develop a higher level of intuition, of psychic and telepathic awareness and also empathic perception.

Although this book is geared to assist you to develop your empathic energies and because part of your development will entail working with your third-eye chakra, it is important to also take a moment to address the benefits of maintaining a healthy and balanced chakra system. The reason for this is that every chakra is connected to each other and together, they create a divine flow of energy. If one of the seven primary chakras is not flowing properly—due to emotional blockages—the flow of energy can be obstructed to the other chakras. In order to optimally activate your third-eye chakra, it would be beneficial for you to become familiar with the six other chakras in the spiritual body. To follow is a brief introduction to the other chakras and their primary function. Beginning at the base of the spine:

• Root Chakra: Represents stability and security
• Sacral Chakra: Represents passion and creativity
• Solar Plexus Chakra: Represents Will power and is seat of emotions

• Heart Chakra: Represents the bridge between lower and higher chakras; the center of love
• Throat Chakra: Expression, Truth and creative channel for the spoken word
• Third Eye Chakra: The Single eye; intuition, divine perception and divine knowingness
• Crown Chakra: Divine Realization and Oneness with God Force; enlightenment

Each of the seven chakras is associated with specific attributes of spiritual maturity and development. Although it is not a requirement for an Empath to develop the chakra system in order to be a vehicle for messages, the quality of energy flow can be greatly obstructed if there are blockages in the chakras, and conversely, the energy flow can be greatly enhanced when the entire chakra system is flowing optimally.

A good analogy to illustrate the importance of healthy chakras is to imagine a large water pipe with several V connections. Imagine that there is a blockage in one or more of the connections. The result will be that the flow of water will be affected by the blockages. Now imagine the blockages being released for the V connections. The release will create an immediate flow of water through the pipe.

There are different theories as to whether a vessel of messages (Empath, Medium, Psychic, Intuitive, and Healer) have an impact on the receipt and delivery of messages and/or healing. Some theories suggest that it does not make a difference whether a vessel is emotionally or spiritually healthy in order to be a messenger for others. In my professional observation, both as a guru and vessel that wears many hats, I advocate that the quality of the vessel's energy is very important to the successful receipt and delivery of divine insight.

Practices to Clear Chakras

• Meditation
• Reconciling The Past
• Spiritual Maintenance

Meditation is a practice that can truly enhance our state of well-being. Many people are intimidated by the practice of meditation because they fear not practicing it correctly. Others feel they do not have the time to devote to a meditation practice. Truthfully, there is no right or wrong way to mediate. And although there are several forms of meditation that can be very powerful, any time devoted to stilling the mind and connecting with the soul can be extremely beneficial to the mind, body and spirit.

It can be very challenging to be an open vessel for others if there is emotional debris within you. On the highest level of empathic work, the energy of love and light are vital components that can enhance both the quality of a reading and the overall experience for both the receiver and the giver. Vibrating from a place of love requires that we are as freed from heavy energies as much as possible. If a vessel is carrying extremes amount of emotional baggage, it may interfere with the development of the sixth sense and also with the quality of readings an Empath is delivering.

Spiritual maintenance is such an important aspect of Empath work. No matter how rewarding a calling to be of service is, it also requires a great deal of energy to be present, to practice awareness and to be an optimal vessel for healing and for giving messages. In truth, we cannot give what we do not have, and although as an Empath, we should not be using our own energies to convey messages, we are still serving as a vessel for holding and transmitting energy. For these reasons, it is very important for the Empath to take the proper time to nourish and nurture themselves by taking the time to receive from others as well. This nurturing can be received through simple pleasures such as massages, healings, pedicures, facials or by simply taking the time to replenish and relax. A "full" vessel will have fuel to give but an empty vessel will feel depleted and this, in turn, can tarnish the delivery of insights and compromise the well-being of an Empath.

The Sixth Sense and Spirituality

It can be challenging to learn about the Sixth Sense without incorporating at some level the practice of Spirituality. While there is no set protocol on needing to practice any form of religious structure, nor is there a prerequisite to be spiritual, when we embrace our spirituality and also recognize it as part of a much greater, Higher Force, we allow ourselves to tap into the infinite source of limitless potentials and possibilities. As we learned in the opening of this lesson, the sixth sense is part of the Chakra system, and this system is part of our spiritual makeup. Thus, it would be natural, then, to have a desire to learn more about our spirituality and

31

to harness our divine nature in order to optimally tap into the Infinite source from where empathic energy truly derives.

The sixth sense invites us to become One with the unified field that connects every living entity to the embodiment of a collective. In this state of awareness, everyone can naturally be aware of the energies of others because they are recognizing that there truly is no separation between ourselves and others. Yes, on a physical level, we are all unique and we all possess characteristics and personality traits that are different, but on a spiritual level, we are all simply molecules of the Oneness that created all.

When we allow our spiritual nature to blossom within the scope of being an Empath, we will quickly find ourselves expanding and growing in our own lives in a more wholesome and fulfilling way and then we will be optimally fueled to ignite the spirit of others by the very fullness that we are experiencing. Remembering the a Empath is primarily vibrating from a field of emotions, imagine the difference that it would make for both the receiver and the giver if the Empath is experiencing a deep sense of wholeness, of purpose and fulfillment as he or she conducts service.

An Empath can still operate and become sensitized to the emotions of others regardless of whether he or she has fully developed their sixth sense, or whether or not they have chosen to expand their spirituality. The difference in the experience will be that when a spiritual foundation is not established, the Empath may only be tapping into the fields of "physicality" and limitations that exists in our world. When the Empath allows the foundation of spirituality to become the core of his or her vibration, there is a great sense of support and expansion that is experienced by the Empath and in turn, can then be offered as a gift to the receivers of messages.

Practices to Develop the Third-Eye Chakra

Meditation: This is a simple meditation that will assist in opening your chakras. Practice it at least every two days or more often if you like.

Begin by sitting comfortably with your eyes closed, and your focused attention on your spine. When you are ready, take a gentle inhale through your nostrils and exhale through the mouth. Wait

a few moments and then take another inhale and
then exhale.

Envision a sphere of golden, white light hovering
over your head. Feel the calmness and peace
that begins to embrace you. As you bring your
attention to the golden sphere, notice that the
top of your head is gently tingling and feeling
expanded. This is your Crown Chakra, the center
of divine insight. Envision the golden light gently
moving through your crown chakra and notice if
you see any colors and objects as the energy
gently expands your chakra. Take a few
moments to feel the freedom of lightness and
peace that you feel.

When you are ready, invite the golden sphere of
light to move downward to your third-eye chakra,
the Empath center. As you feel the energy
expanding your Chakra, allow yourself to feel the
vision of a indigo color to fill your third-eye
chakra. Gently feel the energy expanding,
bringing clarity and peace as it moves through
your centers.

Gently invite the golden energy to move
downward to your throat chakra, the center of
expression. As you experience the golden sphere,
envision a sky blue energy opening the throat
chakra and releasing any debris that may be
present. Feel the light.

When you are ready, envision the sphere moving
to your heart chakra, the center of love. Fill the
golden energy filling your heart center and
expanding it with a luminous green light. Allow

yourself to release any past or present emotional injuries. Become filled with unconditional love.

You are noticing how expanded and open you are feeling. Invite the golden sphere to move to your solar plexus and feel the empowerment of your divine will. Envision a bright yellow light expanding from your center.

Next, invite the golden sphere to gently move downward to your sacral chakra. Feel the expansion and movement of your creative energy; feel the passion of your soul come alive. Envision an orange flame of light, gently moving in this center. Feel the awakening of your soul.

Now, invite the sphere to move downward to your root chakra, the center of stability and ground. Feel the strength of your spirit and envision a red light expanding from this center. Feel the anchoring that you are receiving from the earth. You are stable and strong.

Take a moment to notice that you have become a rainbow of colors. The golden sphere has gently activated and opened your 7 chakra centers. Bathe yourself in the loving, golden light as you also envision the expansion of your chakras. Feel the balance of your new energy.

Exercise for Clearing the Past

In a notebook or journal, begin by making a list of names of people—past or present—who you feel you hold any heavy emotional energy towards. It could be the energy of anger, of betrayal, deep disappointment, etc. Once you complete the list of names, circle the ones that ignite the greatest amount of emotion in you right now. Once you have done this, turn to a clean page and begin to write a pardon letter to this individual. The scope of the pardon letters is to allow you to release any harbored emotions that you have from any emotional and painful experiences.

This exercise is for your SELF-HEALING and as such, there is NO need to give the pardon letters to the individuals. You can even write one to individuals who have passed. There is an incredible healing process that takes place when we write pardon letters.

There is no right or wrong way to compose a pardon letter. You can be an expressive and honest as you need to be, taking the time to first highlight your feelings, your disappointments, etc. The KEY of the pardon letters is to finally reach a state of rendering pardon to the individuals, knowing that when you do, you will be creating an amazing release of emotional space in your soul to experience new and happier moments.

Compose a pardon letter for everyone that you circled in your list of names. Once you have reached a point where you have completed released them, you can discard the letters.

If you are inspired, you can conduct pardon letters to the individuals in your list that you did not circle as an added inspiration for your wholeness and healing

Chapter 4

Journaling and Empathy

Journaling can be a wonderful part of your spiritual and healing development. The process of journaling allows you to deeply reach those intimate places within our soul that hold our deepest feelings and truth, and it allows you to safely and freely express them. Journaling can be very healing because it invites you to be naked about your feelings without the fear of being judged or ridiculed. A journal is like an old, trusted friend; it listens intently to every single expression you have without interruptions, does not judge you and often can reveal guidance and direction.

A journal can also serve as a navigational tool because at times when you are submerged in your deepest emotions, you may not be completely aware of what our emotions and feelings are pointing to; a direction, an answer that you have been searching for, that may very well be captured somewhere in your journal entries. Many individuals, who keep journals, have stumbled on many realizations by simply reading old entries.

For an Empath, journal writing can not only be a navigational tool but also can serve as a guide to help in interpreting messages. It can also hold— much like a library full of books---all the records of insights that you have experienced that can reveal a certain technique or pattern that may be presented in your readings. This can be very important especially in the beginning of your empathic development. As we discovered in a previous chapter, Empaths can use one or more of their five senses to receive insight. A journal is a perfect place to record your impressions and observations as you harness your empathic abilities.

A great way to use a journal as an Empath tool is to offer a close friend or family member a reading and after you are done, take some time to notice which and how many of your five senses did you find yourself tapping into as you conducted the reading? A journal that is dedicated to your Empath development can be divided to include several sections:

• Check-list of five senses/readings
• Observations on your development
• Meditations/Chakra development work for your sixth sense
• Validations that you have received from empathic readings/insights

As you begin to record the data on your insights in your journal, you will discover that keeping track of your development can also give you a sense of what your style of empathy work is. You may discover that you are a seer or a feeler by the observation of your entry notes as you begin to practice and sharpen your empathic nature.

Dreams and Premonitions

Dreams and premonitions can also be a part of an Empath's path to develop and harness his or her energies. Before I discuss these two modalities of empathy, let me first discuss each one individually.

Dreams are a mystery to some and a portal for messages to others. Dreams are sometimes random and obscure; with no rhyme or reason. Other times, dreams are a result of a conscious or subconscious thought or experience that was present and weighing in our minds. They can sometimes be triggered by an event, something that was watched in the news, a movie or a conversation that has taken place. And many times, dreams make absolutely no sense whatsoever.

For the Empath, dreams may be a means by which to receive messages. Most of the time, it is not the actual events that are being shown in a dream that are literal, but more so, the "Feeling" and the people who are involved in the dream. A hypothetical example of this would be that an Empath dreams that a friend is jumping out of an airplane and experiences anxiety as he is getting ready to jump. The dream may be revealing that this person is afraid of heights or of moving forward; but not literally that he is going to jump out of a plane. The goal of an Empath is to capture the "feeling" and the deeper meaning of what an action of a dream is revealing. Here, again, there is no "right or wrong" way to interpret a dream; a dream may have one meaning for someone and an entirely different interpretation for another.

Using your journal to post your dreams can be a very helpful tool in assisting you to learn how to tap deeper into the interpretation of your dreams. In time, you may discover that certain scenes in your dreams may represent a unique language that is only exclusive to your empathic nature. Your journal can be the record-keeper of any repetitive or significant style of messaging that may be coming through the state of dreaming. For this reason, refrain from looking outside of yourself for interpretation of your dreams. Sit and journal your memories of any dreams and spend time studying them; seeing if there is a distinctive pattern, scene or feeling that always accompanies your dreaming state. Notice how you feel after a dream; do you feel heightened, anxious, or anticipatory? Capture all of your feelings as you also capture all the details of your dreams.

Premonitions are strong feelings that surface about an upcoming event or situation. Premonitions are considered to be messages that come in advance regarding a future event or situation. This style of empathy can often be labeled under the umbrella of being "psychic" but in my professional observation, there is a difference between a psychic and an Empath that has premonitions. The difference is usually measured in the way the messages are received. For a psychic, messages may usually surface when they are having a direct contact with someone that they are engaging with. For the Empath, the messages of premonitions may surface even when a reading is not taking place. A Empath may be walking in a supermarket or in a park and suddenly feel a sensation as though she or he has been transported to another state of consciousness and with no warning, may begin to see a premonition.

The premonition may give the Empath a feeling that she or he is watching a short scene of a movie on a screen. Some Empaths describe the feeling similar to having a dream but in a wakeful state. There are some Empaths that actually experience deep sensations in their bodies and in their five senses as they are viewing a premonition. Oftentimes, there is a feeling of "returning to the body" after a premonition, as if the Empath was transported to another dimension; an altered state of reality. In truth, there are many levels of dimensions that are operating at the same time in different levels of frequency. An Empath may naturally develop these higher states of knowingness or may be born with these natural abilities, and finally, may not need to develop them at all because it is not part of their divine matrix to do so.

What is important is for the Empath to gently learn how to know his or herself in a subtle but progressive way. It is also important to not get caught up in the many labels that attempt to define the many aspects of "Empathy" or any other modality that is truly a gift from our spirit. By learning to listen to your feelings and to develop your own unique language that will help you to interpret your messages, you will discover that you are going to be your greatest teacher. In the interim, journal writing will greatly assist you to become the explorer and the reporter of your experiences. Journaling is one of the most important tools that you will use in learning how to harness your empathic nature because it will hold for you all of your experiences, discoveries, observations and feelings as you move ahead.

41

As we complete this chapter and continue on to the exercises, it would be beneficial for you to purchase a couple of journals or notebooks. While traditional journals can be very trendy and pretty, I actually find that a five-subject notebook also works very well in complimenting the several sections that you will ideally create in your journal.

Sectioning Journal

Your journal/notebook should have at least five sections:

• Everyday entries/Impressions
• Observations of the Five Senses During Readings
• Meditations/Charka Development of the Sixth Sense
• Dreams
• Premonitions

Maintain your journal for the next 5 days. On the sixth day, answer the questions below:

• Have you created a bond with your journal? Yes No
• Do you find it difficult to journal? Yes No
• Do you remember having any dreams? Yes No
• Was there anything repetitive about the dreams?
 Yes No
• Have you experienced any premonitions? Yes No

Read your journal entries for the last five days. With a highlighter, note any new experiences or discoveries that you have made about your style of Empathic nature.

Assignment: I would like you to compose a 300-600 word essay of what you have learned about yourself and your Empathic nature since you began this book. Be as simple and authentic as you possibly can and also be as detailed as possible with any areas that you are being challenged with. Share what your progress has been with the exercises and your meditations. Also include in your essay, the responses to the five questions listed above. You can include them at the end of your essay.

At the end of your essay, you also have the opportunity to ask a specific question on an area or concern that you may have or are experiencing as you harness your empathic nature. Once you have completed the essay, you are welcomed to send it to me via email at spirituality1@aol.com

I will revise your essay and respond to your question as promptly as I can and will offer any suggestions that may be helpful. I look forward to hearing from you!

Chapter 5

Strengthening The Empathic Muscle

Working on strengthening your empathic muscle is much like working any other part of your body; if you work it out, it gets stronger and more defined and if you do not, it becomes sluggish and weak. We know that to work out the body requires devotion and commitment and that is exactly what you need to do in order to get your empathic muscle stronger.

There are a variety of ways that you can strengthen your empathic muscle and all it requires is for you to have devotion to putting in the time and patience. Just like any workout, it takes practice to build the muscles and it also takes time. Feelings of impatience and frustration will only interfere with your commitment to practice and build your empathic muscle and it will also take the fun out of the experience.

Expectations are another energy that can surely interfere with your development process. I like to use the analogy of when we were children, learning the alphabets, how impossible it seemed to have to memorize 26 letters! Now, as adults, we don't even remember how much work it took for us to remember the order of the alphabets. The same truth holds for learning how to harness your empathic energies. In the beginning, it may seem like an impossible task to remember to apply and practice all of the principles that have been introduced to you.

At times, it may feel frustrating that you are not noticing any changes in the heightening of your awareness, but in truth, every moment that you apply to strengthening your empathic muscle will count. Having expectations will only serve to disappoint and to discourage you from working hard towards your goal.

In order to strengthen your empathic muscle it is also important for you to take the time to nurture and nourish yourself emotionally, mentally, physically and spiritually. In an earlier chapter you learned the importance of releasing old emotional debris from the past. As you continue to work on harnessing your empathic energy, it is important to take the steps that will insure that you are keeping yourself mentally and emotionally healthy.

By practicing your affirmations and also the principle of lovingly detachment, you will insure that you are not being depleted by any surrounding energies and keeping your vessel full of divine energy. For your physical wellbeing, it is important to eat a healthy and balanced diet, to drink plenty of pure water and to also include a regimen of exercise that will bring vitality to the body. The body is the vessel that holds the divine energy that allows you to receive insight, it is important, then, to take care of your body and to keep it strong and healthy. Your commitment to your mental, emotional and physical wellbeing will greatly assist your spiritual body.

One of the greatest ways to nurture and fortify your soul is to include a healthy dose of nature and outdoor activities as part of your wellness regimen. Nature is so very nurturing to the soul because it feeds the very essence of your soul with pure energy. Taking walks in a park, lake or beach can be a wonderful way to strengthen your spiritual muscle and to receive replenishment and restorative energy. Flowers and animals are also very healing and fortifying to the soul. If you have a zoo or garden nearby, take the time to be in the company of flowers and the animals and see how calm and rejuvenated you will feel.

The sun has powerful rays of energy and healing properties. The gentle warmth of the sun and its golden hue energy are known to rejuvenate and replenish the mind, the body and spirit. Just ten minutes of bathing in the sun is all that is needed to receive the nourishment and energy that the sun can provide. It is important to be discerning and to apply sun block whenever you expose yourself to the sun and to also drink plenty of fresh water. However, there is something incredibly soothing and replenishing about taking in the sun's rays—especially for energy workers—because the sun is a burst of energy as well!

An Empath taps into and utilizes an immense amount of energy in order to be a vessel for messages. The reasons are varied. One of the greatest reasons is that sometimes the energy of the receiver is heavy and in some way, interferes with the reception that an Empath is attempting to tap in to. Other times, it is because there are other people around or the environment is heavy. By heavy, I mean that there are lower vibration energies; loud music, yelling, screaming, laughing, gossiping, Television sounds, etc. In order for an Empath to create a reception, he or she must raise their vibration to a very high state. The Empath uses his or her energy to raise themselves to a higher frequency; this takes mental and physical energy to do.

Some helpful suggestions that can assist an Empath in reserving his/her energy while offering reading are:

• Make sure that you are well rested and replenished before offering a reading
• Take a few minutes to center yourself, to Inhale and to Exhale God Force energy
• Light a candle to create a field of calmness and tranquility
• Burn Sage; it is a purifying and healing herb
• Turn off electronics: TV, radio, cell phones, etc.
• If there are people in the room, ask them to please be silent while you do a reading
• Drink plenty of water before and during the reading
• Refrain from drinking alcoholic beverages before or during a reading
• Hold a gemstone such as a white quartz to amplify the clear reception

The use of gemstone can be very helpful and useful not only in offering readings but also to keep you grounded and focused. Grounding is another way of strengthening or anchoring a field of energy. When I offer Afterlife events, I use white quartz as a reception tool. Before I begin the readings, I give everyone a little pouch that contains a white quartz. I ask everyone to place a little greeting note in the pouch to a beloved past one and then I collect the pouches. When I am ready, I begin by selecting a pouch and connecting to the gemstone—that now has been activated by the individual who touched it and who placed a message in the pouch. The quartz serves as an antenna as well as a connecting tool for the field, the person and for me.

Gemstones can also be a wonderful grounding tool that can help the Empath to strengthen a field of energy and to ground their own field of energy when they are opening a field. All gemstones have a very unique quality and attribute. Some of my favorite grounding stones are Red jasper and Tigers Eye. Both of these stones are very earthy and are favorites among Shamans and light-workers who do healing and grounding work.

Gemstones can be worn as jewelry, but truly, their purpose is much more than to accessorize attire. In ancient times, amulets and sacred jewelry was worn with very specific reasons. Shamans, Medicine Doctors, Healers and Deities knew that part of their divine garb was to include powerful gemstones pieces that would assist in holding certain frequencies, create a protective shield of energy around them and also carry powerful healing properties that would assist them in offering healing.

Although there is a science to gemstones and their properties, I also invite people to allow themselves to be drawn to specific stones naturally. This process is very simple. If you are shopping for gemstones, take the time to feel the energy of certain stones. See if you are attracted to a particular one by its size or color. Read the information on the properties of the stone and see if it resonates with a need that your soul may have and that it wishes to fortify or strengthen with a specific property value that a stone offers. Pay attention to your feelings and trust them. Once you have found your stones, you should then take the time to become intimate with them. Sit and meditate with them, talk to them and ask for their assistance. It may sound silly to be talking to a stone but truthfully, gemstones are alive and full of vibrant energy.

As you can see, working on strengthening your empathic muscle primarily encompasses taking time to truly take care of yourself by conducting nourishing practices that will not only fortify your empathic nature but also benefit your overall state of spiritual wellness. Empaths love to give of themselves to others and in order to be an optimal vessel, an Empath has to also be able to give to his or herself—and this should be the first order of protocol, because when you are a full vessel, then, you have plenty to offer and to give to others.

Exercises

You are going to be a Empathic reporter for yourself with the next two exercises. In your journal, create a new section entitled: Strengthening Exercises, or if you prefer, get a new journal just dedicated for this part of your development. In a fresh page, begin by writing the first day of the week, "Monday" and then skip a few pages in your journal and continue to create a section for each day of the week.

Exercise 1

At least two or three times a week, make an effort to take at least 10 minutes to either:

• Take a stroll in the park or the beach
• Connect with nature; visit a garden or zoo
• Take in the sun for 10-15 minutes

If you have the time, take your journal with you and immediately after indulging yourself in your nourishing and strengthening activity, take a few minutes to jot down where you went and how did it make you feel. Listen to your body and notice if you feel calmer, more in-tune with yourself or if you notice that your senses are heightened. Also notice if you feel more relaxed after your activity and if you sleep better during the night. Finally, also take note of any heightened awareness that follows your activity such as vivid dreams, visions, etc.

*It is important that you journal your entries on the particular day that it takes place because the goal is to remind yourself that YOU NEED to make time for these activities. By making a section for each day of the week, you will be inspired to make time to do them more than once in a while. Remember, that working on your Empathic muscle is like going to the gym to work out your physical muscles; if you only go once in a while, it will take a very long time to experience any real results.

Exercise 2

Conduct a little investigating and locate a reputable gemstone shop that carries a variety of stones.

Select a day to visit the shop and make it an exciting event. If you can, visit the shop by yourself and take along a pocket notebook and pen.

When you arrive to the shop, take your time feeling the space and energy. If it feels light and inviting, move to the stones and begin to get acquainted with the different varieties. Do not be afraid to take your time, taking notice of both the size and color of the stones as well as the energetic feel that each one has.

Next, educate yourself on the properties of each stone. Most shops display stones in little boxes and have a label that features the qualities of the stones. If the shop you are visiting does not provide a display with the qualities of the stones, do not be afraid to ask!

In your notebook, jot down any impressions that you are picking up. Is there a particular stone that you are drawn to? Jot down the name of the stone and color and also the qualities in your notebook. Continue to jot down any impressions for as many stones as you feel drawn to.

It is not necessary to feel obligated to purchase any stones if you are not drawn to any or if you are not sure. Purchase one or more if you feel drawn to them. And, if you pick up more than one, prioritize them in order of attraction: "Really loved the Citrine, liked the Jasper." etc.

Also explore any gemstone jewelry pieces and see if there is one that you are really drawn to. It does not matter if the jewelry is a bracelet, necklace or ring, and it does not have to be an expensive piece in order for it to serve you. What is important is that you are drawn to it. If you like a particular piece of jewelry and elect to purchase it, take note of how you feel when you wear it.

Chapter 6

Trusting the Messages

One of the most challenging aspects of harnessing your Empathic energy is learning how to trust the messages that you receive. The attribute of trust is surely one that will take patience to harness and it will blossom as you gain confidence in your abilities and fully begin to embrace your gift.

In the beginning, many Empaths find it difficult to acknowledge that they have an amazing gift. It is easier to assume that "everyone has the abilities to feel the emotions of others" than to admit that there is something uniquely special about ourselves. For some Empaths, declaring themselves equates to expressing a level of arrogance or specialness above others. And yet, without the ability to fully embrace and to declare yourself, your gifts as an Empath may be limited from the immense potential that it can have in assisting and guiding others. This is why it is so important for you to trust yourself and to also learn how to trust the messages you receive.

One of the greatest fears that some Empaths experience is of delivering a wrong message. "What if the message is inaccurate?" When I am offering a reading, before I begin, I always inform the individual that I am "Only a messenger." I also remind them that they should only "Accept what resonates and to leave what does not." In making this declaration to the receiver, I am setting the stage to advise them that they may not agree with some of the insights that I am providing and that if this happens, it is perfectly OK. As an Empath, our job is not to convince someone to accept the messages we are providing or to attempt to deliver the messages that a receiver would like to hear. Our job is to focus on the messages that manifest and to convey them as clearly and as authentically as we can—without having any expectations—but also with tactfulness and discernment.

In order to learn how to deepen your ability to trust the messages and insights that you receive, it is important to remove yourself completely from any traces of:

• Assumption
• Conclusion
• Expectation
• Outcome

An Empath should refrain from making assumptions about a message. Let us look at an example: Say that you are getting a message for someone to become a teacher but as you receive the message, you realize that the person has six little ones at home and that it will be impossible for her to go to school to earn her teaching degree...do not assume...just deliver the message. Perhaps it may seem impossible for this individual to attend school but remember that if a soul has a desire to fulfill, then, the opportunity for the fulfillment of this goal also exists!

Continuing to use the example above, it is important to honor a message even though you may not always clearly understand how the message is going to be fulfilled. An Empath's responsibility is not to provide step-by-step instructions on how someone is going to ultimately fulfill a soul's calling; the path and destination is exactly what the soul desires to experience besides the actual realization of the goal. If you are shown insight on certain steps that should be taken in order for someone to fulfill a goal, then, by all means, share it. However, feeling an obligation to provide a conclusion to a soul's invitation to explore an avenue is not what an Empath does—An Empath is a messenger, not a coordinator or event planner.

Expectations in readings can be a great challenge for the Empath. Sometimes expectations are presented from both the receiver of the messages and also by the Empath. From the receiving side, most people have high expectations of what it is that they desire to hear when having a reading. Most people want to know specific details about career, relationships, the future, etc. My personal and professional observation in this issue is that Spirit will not always reveal what someone wants to know...but more importantly, Spirit will address and highlight the issues and areas of life that are MOST important in the present moment that will optimally provide the greatest potential for healing, growth and expansion for an individual.

One of the greatest expectations that most people have when receiving a reading is found in wanting a guarantee for a specific outcome in a given situation. Say, for example, someone that you are reading is given the message that they should seriously evaluate the status of their relationship. Say the message allures to being unhappy in the relationship and that serious consideration about the relationship should be explored. Immediately, the person receiving the message may want to know if:

• Is the relationship going to definitely end?
• Are they going to find another partner soon after?
• Is their partner going to get involved in another relationship quickly?

Observing the example above, notice that the message delivered was to "evaluate and consider" the current status of a relationship. The message is not offering any specific outcome but more so, highlighting an area that needs attention. However, from the receiver's perspective, the invitation to "explore" has been completely overshadowed by the desire to know the outcome of the situation—leaving a crucial piece of the puzzle out---the need to "explore!"

By having an expectation to immediately know the outcome, a receiver may completely overlook the real message of a situation—which is to become aware and to focus on addressing a current situation rather than by-passing it. As an Empath, we may feel pressured and obligated to please a receiver by providing the answers to expectations and outcomes that are not currently being revealed. However disappointed a receiver may feel, it is crucial for an Empath to honor and to trust that what is being revealed is exactly what needs to be heard and addressed in the moment of now.

A Seer versus a Creator

In my own readings, I always remind a receiver that I am only a Seer. but that every receiver is a divine Creator. The reason why it is so important for me to remind them of this truth is because a Seer; an Empath, can only "see" what is being projected in the matrix of the "moment of now." And, although an Empath can also possess the ability to be precognizant (the ability to see into the future), the ultimate truth is that as Creators, a receiver can choose to recreate—whether consciously or unconsciously--his or her future in a moment, merely by making another choice! For this powerful reason, an Empath can only deliver the message—the seed of potential...but the receiver must then choose to feed the seed with intention in order to harness it to manifestation.

Trust the Messages

There have been countless of times when I have "seen" something in a person's photograph when working on photo sessions that has challenged my knowingness. In a recent session, I was tapping into the individual's field and suddenly I felt the energy of a horse! I was a bit fatigued after a long day of sessions and almost chose to disregard the message. As I was jotting down my impressions, I felt the energy of the horse again and knew that I had to trust my feelings. As I wrote my email report to the client, I told her that she had an intense connection to horses and that their energy was very healing for her. It was a blissful validation when the client wrote back in complete awe to share with me that she had always loved horses and that just recently, she had been inspired to go on a weekend retreat to a horse ranch and had an incredible healing experience while riding a horse!

The most incredible experience I have had with the principle of trust and Empathic work occurred when I first began my holistic practice and was working with a client on a pictorial exercise that I created to help clients connect to their intuitive soul's messages. The exercise called for clients to randomly choose 10 magazine photos for ten very specific questions that would be posed to their spirit. I would then sit with the photo exercise and connect with the energy of each image and also with the specific question posed to their spirit.

I was working with a client who had come to me with a severe MS (Multiple Sclerosis) condition and who was simply attempting to receive some pain relieve through holistic healing. I invited her to do the pictorial exercise and in one of the images, I could feel that the client had a very gifted ability to paint. I shared my insight with the client and she rebutted my suggestion. The client, ironically, worked as an intellectual professional in a high caliber executive position. I gently presented the message again and this time, she admitted that as a child, she had been inspired to paint, but that she was discouraged by her parents to pursue an artistic passion because it would fail to produce a stable financial future. And, so, she abandoned her desire to paint.

I encouraged to give it a try again since it has been proven that artistic energy can be a form of healing therapy. To her surprise, on her first attempt, she created a magnificent painting of a mountain. What was even more amazing was that the client continued to paint and as she did, she began to demonstrate an amazing healing transformation with her MS. In a short time, the client was completely off medications and completely free of pain. Not only did she heal from her physical aliment, but was also able to truly connect to her soul's passion of painting and to become a meditation teacher. To this day, I remind myself of that fateful reading and know that it has served me as a crucial foundation in trusting the messages and insight that come through—even when a client is not resonating with it. At the end, each client has the ability to accept the message if it resonates or to reject it. But for the Empath, the ability to unconditionally trust the message and to deliver it can make all the difference in the world for a client!

Exercise

Part 1

• How Do You Feel about Trusting the Messages you receive?
• Have you ever questioned your Empathic gift?
• In your experience working with individuals, which of following has been the most challenging for you?

- Assumption
- Conclusion
- Expectation
- Outcome

After you have answered the questions, what have you learned about yourself and trusting your intuitive insight?

Part 2

Arrange to present at least 3 reading to friends or family members. Before you begin, get a notebook for your readings and create 3 sections for each of your readings. In the first page of each section, create a category for the following: Assumption, Conclusion, Expectation and Outcome. Make sure to leave space in between each category for comments.

As you conduct your readings, take note of the categories and observe if you are experiencing challenges with any of them. Also make note of any observations you are receiving from the client in reference to the category subjects: Are they pushing for a conclusion, do they have expectations or are they asking for an outcome? Jot it all down.

After you have completed your readings, ask each individual if they would please offer you an authentic review of the reading they received. This can be done by giving them a clean sheet of paper and asking them to write a brief paragraph of their experience. Ask them to share if they were pleased with the reading and also if they were "expecting more" "hoping for a more specific message" or "desiring a more "defined outcome" to share your experience---and have fun exploring!

Chapter 7

Presenting Messages in a Positive Light

As an Empath, one of our greatest goals is to be able to deliver messages as authentically as possible. Another goal should be to aim at presenting messages in a positive light, introducing inspiration and hope, no matter what the messages are potentially revealing. I emphasize the word "potential" because as we have learned in the previous lesson, an Empath is a Seer but the receivers are divine Creators and with this empowering attribute, they can potentially chose to recreate any experience and bring it to a higher level of potential outcome. This process of recreating can be greatly encouraged by an Empath as she or he delivers messages, offering the reminder of the potency of creative intention and manifestation.

There are certain ways of presenting information with tactfulness, discernment, compassion and optimism. Of course, there are also ways of introducing insight with limitations, with rawness and fear. Thus, the presentation of a reading can leave a receiver feeling positive and hopeful or it can leave them feeling helpless, hopeless and fearful. It is all a matter of where an Empath is choosing to vibrate from; if the Seer is operating from a state of positive or negative energy...and trust me, it can make all the difference in the world to a receiver.

It is important to recognize that although people may seek to receive readings for entertainment purposes, most are likely doing so because they are feeling stuck, confused or emotionally distraught in a given situation within lives. And if distress is not present, people will still, most likely, approach the reading with a state of vulnerability; feeling anxious or anticipatory about what a reader is going to "see and say." This is why it is very important to practice sensitivity and discernment when offering readings.

I like to compare readings to a diagnosis that a doctor may render a patient. In some instances, a doctor may use tactfulness and sensitive even when he or she is delivering an unpleasant diagnosis. The doctor may offer alternatives and treatments that may immediately create a sense of hope and optimism for the patient. On the other hand, there are doctors who have lost their sense of sensitivity and when they deliver a diagnosis, they have forgotten to be mindful of the power that they may potentially have on a patient when rendering a diagnosis. The delivery of a diagnosis—and a reading can be a curse or a blessing---because the "word has great power" and just one word can disempowered or empower someone.

Introducing messages in a positive light requires optimism, compassion and faith; and it also requires detachment from our own personal perspective of a situation or scenario —especially if it is based on a past personal experience.

I recently was a witness to a reading where the Reader did not practice any of the principles above. I knew the Reader; she was an old client of mine. Years prior, she had sought counseling because she was in a very unhappy marriage with a very aggressive man. She was afraid to end the marriage because she feared he would hurt her and their children. She also feared that he would not honor child support and that he would basically move on and forget the children. Gracefully, we worked hard to help her release her fears and she was able to successfully move through her divorce without any major consequences.

Years later, my old client contacted me to tell me she was offering Tarot card readings. I felt that a very close student of mine could benefit from a reading because she had been in the process of contemplating a separation from her husband. We arranged a reading and my student requested that I be present. Within minutes of the reading beginning, I wanted to stop it. I immediately recognized that the reader was projecting her own bitter experiences of her divorce onto the receiver. As much as I wanted to interfere, I also knew that my student had to have the experience for a reason. By the end of the reading, my student was horrified. The Reader had triggered all of her fears and had offered very little optimism for the future.

Luckily, I was aware of the projection that the Reader was placing on the student and how she failed to offer a reading from a place of detachment. At the end, we must honor that there is always a gift in every experience. For my student, it was a strong reminder that we should not allow others to disempower us, nor should we accept something as "Truth" if it does not resonate in our hearts. Ironically, the Reader also served a purpose. Her role was to trigger the student's greatest fears and to bring them to the surface. However, the end result could have been very different if my student was not evolved enough to recognize that she had a choice to perceive the messages from a state of positive light; to recognize that the Reader was simply a trigger for her to recognize and embrace her own fears.

In my observation, the Reader lacked compassion and the capability to vibrate from a heart-centered place that could offer hope and alternatives rather than to provoke fear and a sense of helplessness in the receiver. No matter what a reader sees, the introduction of light and of hope can always be introduced and it can make all the difference in the world, to the receiver and also to the future success of a Seer.

There are questions that can arise when we consider that an Empath should "be lovingly detached" and still honor the protocols to also be:

• Authentic with the messages
• Emotionally able to convey the messages
• Offer positive light and guidance without tainting the message

The **key** is to remember that what an Empath "sees" is not necessarily set in stone and that by offering a positive delivery of messages and guidance, an Empath can "encourage" the receiver to create new thoughts and intentions that can recreate and shift the potential of an "outcome" to a higher positive one.

Being authentic does not mean that we have to be crude. The delivery of messages can always be adorned with compassion and subtleness and also with the invitation for a receiver to tap into the resources of creating powerful intentions that can bring about a shift in any potential experience. By emphasizing on the word "potential," we can celebrate the divine truth that nothing is set in stone just because a "Seer" is observing something and it also invites the receiver to step into a place of empowerment and action to create a higher outcome.

It is important to practice lovingly detachment when delivering messages. Our own personal history and experiences should not influence the readings we are providing. No two situations are ever alike because each soul has a unique "agenda" as to why it is choosing to have an experience. If an Empath cannot separate his or her own personal feelings about a given situation, a reading can be tainted with the personal emotional energy of the Empath.

Presenting messages from a positive light does not mean that we have to adhere to any specific religious belief or dogma, but rather, that we operate from a heart-centered place that offers the energies of compassion, of love and opportunities for expansion and growth. There is such a wonderful feeling of exchange when we are able to arm someone with a sense of hope and empowerment and when we also lovingly offer the invitation to seek alternatives or solutions rather than to crudely make prophecies with a deep conviction of finality, as if there was no other choice in the matter.

At the end, the greatest gift that an Empath possesses is the ability to guide someone who may be "lost in the forest" by outlining that there is indeed several paths that can lead them out to a place of freedom. And that, although the experience of "feeling lost" may give the impression of feeling helpless and alone, there is always a great force within that is guiding us through every moment of every experience, leading us to a higher state of experience and growth.

The final analysis should be whether we desire to contribute to someone's growth potential and offer them readings that can leave them feeling empowered with choices and optimism, or do we choose to strip someone of their strength and powerful ability to be divine creators? By introducing a positive light in your field of energy, you can offer a "lantern that can guide others with love and light."

Writing Assignment

Have you ever had a reading where you experienced a negative energy/delivering from a reader? How did it make you feel? Were the messages accurate? Did you feel disempowered or empowered? What did you learn from the experience as a receiver?

Chapter 8

Sharing Your Intuitive Nature with Others

There is no greater feeling for an Empath than to be able to share the gift of Empathy with others and to witness the shifts and transformation that usually follow after a reading. An immense sense of fulfillment and purpose is achieved when we have received validation for the messages that we have offered because it confirms that Empathic work is truly a divine gift that is meant to be shared.

For some Empaths, even after they have taken the time to harness and develop their skills, it is still difficult to "come out of the closet" for a variety of reasons:

• Fear of being ridiculed or of being mocked
• Mistrust in their abilities; fear of being wrong
• Not sure how to branch out

In ancient times, mystics were esteemed as sacred oracles and held distinguished positions in the courts of Kings, Queens and pharaohs. As society descended and separated itself from the Divine Source, Seers, prophets and the likes were viewed as evil people and were judged and prosecuted for the sharing their gifts. Since then, as spirituality continues to emerge, there has been an expansion in the acceptance of many mystical modalities—but there is still a sense of mockery and ridicule that is expressed among many—especially for those who have a strong religious conviction. Still, not since the Ancient times, has there been such a thirst for spiritual understanding and guidance! This is good news for the modern Empath.

The greatest stance that an Empath can take amidst the ridicule and mockery is to stand firmly behind their authentic truth. As long as you are devoted to your truth and are courageous enough to share it, there will always be those who will feel your light and love and who will be drawn to you and opened to receive your guidance and insight. The key, then, is to have the courage to put yourself out there and to let others experience you. It is not always easy to step out into the world, especially when we lack the trust and confidence in our abilities. It is important, then, to practice and to gain confidence in your skills.

Some simple ways to build confidence in your Empathic Energies is to:

• Practice with friends and family

Continue your practice with friends and family as a means to keeping your Empathic muscle strong and active. Even though you are practicing with loved ones who you know, challenge yourself to reach to new heights with them, opening the field to tap into their dream states, their new goals or visions. This is a wonderful way to share and to keep yourself fluid in your skill.

• Ask friends and family to host an Empathic party

This is a fabulous way to begin to branch out in a safe and comfortable way. If a family or friend hosts a Empathic reading on your behalf, it creates a door of recommendation and it acts as a "review" of sorts, that a friend or family member is validating the quality of your work.

• Begin an internship and offer free readings

Offering free readings is a great way to expand your practice and to share. Ideally, your free readings should be offered as an introductory reading; a demo of what a full reading would be like. You can offer sample readings for 10 minutes and then share that a full reading will be longer and more in-depth.

•Create a newsletter and offer free or discounted readings

If you feel that you would like to expand your Empathic gifts to a vocation or professional service, one of the first things you should consider is to create a web site and to offer a newsletter subscription. Creating a presence on the WWW will take some real devotion, time and some financial investment but it is truly the greatest way to advertise services in our modern time of technology.

In the beginning, you may want to start small and to team up with a good and reasonable domain server that offers simple and easy to use formatting to use so that you can create your own website. In time, as your audience expands, you can then consider hiring a professional designer to create a more sophisticated website for you.

• Begin a blog and share your Empathic experiences

In today's modern technology of Ipads, Notebooks and Iphones, it seems that everyone is tuning in to the Internet for up-to-the-moment trends and information. Blogs are a great way to share your voice with audiences and to build a platform in a specific area of profession.

• Join or start a group that centers on Empathic work

It may be surprising to discover how many people are empathic in nature but live in isolation because they do not have a forum to share their thoughts and experiences with. A wonderful way to create a support system and to also advocate awareness and insight on the subject of empathy would be to start a local group in your community, to search for liked mind individuals on the WWW or to become part of an existing group or chapter. It is a great way to meet friends and to get yourself known by the mystic/holistic/spiritual communities.

• Consider writing a book on the subject of Empathy

People love to read books and to hear about real-life stories. For me, writing as served as an amazing platform to share the many hats that I wear under the holistic/spiritual arena. The wonderful thing about writing is that there is no right or wrong way of expression; you can be as simple or as complex as you choose to be, according to the targeted audience that you wish to reach. Books are very inspiring to readers and often trigger them to get in touch with a deeper part of themselves that is yearning to be expressed. I love to write and to share and I also immensely enjoy hearing all the wonderful ways in which my books have impacted and inspired readers in so many ways.

• Connect your empathic work with any other holistic/spiritual work that you offer.

As I mention above, my guru/teacher/counselor hats literally opened the doors for the Empathic and Medium hats to surface. As an author and guru, I found it easier to introduce my empathic work to the core audience that was already familiar with my practice. However, although this seemed to give me an advantage, it also fed into my lack of confidence because it led me to feel that I was only being successful in my readings because I had already built a relationship with the people I was offering readings to. My true moment of "coming out of the closet" arrived when I courageously decided to schedule my first public event! Although I knew that my followers would attend the event, I also knew that it would draw new people...and frankly, I was anxious and very nervous!

In preparation for the event, I practiced many of the insights and tools that have been presented in this book. I took the time to nourish myself spiritually; to meditate and to fuel myself with nurturing energy by spending time outdoors and communing with nature. I reminded myself to remove and release the elements of expectations and obligation and to concentrate on just being a vehicle for Divine energy. I also incorporated the use of a tool—a white quartz—to use as a receptor to connect with the attendees and also to help create a bridge between the subtle energies and the receiver. Finally, before beginning the event, I took a deep breath and surrendered all my fears, cleared my mind and heart and aligned myself with the knowingness that I was a vessel of service.

In my second public event, I became aware that I needed to concentrate more on just being a vessel for those who were willing and ready to receive messages. I share this, because at my second event, there were several attendees that although desperate to receive messages, they were also carrying a lot of emotional blockages that served as a barrier for them to be read.

There was also a gentleman in the audience that was very skeptical and condensing and sitting almost directly across from me. I noticed his energy before I began the readings and I allowed myself to become distracted by his frequency. Thankfully, I was able to discern what was occurring and I re-directed my energies to merge with a higher field of cosmic and divine energies. Although I did experience some anxiety, as soon as I began to read the first person, all the fears and distractions were absorbed by the energy of light and love. The evening was a smashing success and at the end of it, I realized that it is all a matter of practice and trust!

As you can see, there are many wonderful and

simple ways to share your Empathic energy with others while allowing yourself the time to mature and develop in your way and comfort zone. No matter how you chose to share your beautiful gift, there is one thing that is certain; it will bring you much joy and fulfillment! After all, you were given this incredible gift for a reason—to share it!

Questions to ask Yourself

• Do I desire to further develop my abilities in order to share my gift with others?
• How do I envision this happening?
• Do I want to do this as a hobby or do I desire to turn this into a vocation?
• which ideas/suggestions presented in this chapter appealed to me the most?

In Closing

The Joy of Intuition

Intuition is one of the greatest gifts that we can harness and experience as we are partaking in the journey of life. It is the one attribute that reminds us that we are more than just humans, having a spiritual experience. Intuition is the gateway that allows us to truly savor our divine nature!

There are those who believe that intuition is nothing more than an intellectual by-product of reasoning through deduction of logical thought. I say, how sad for those who do not allow themselves to expand their consciousness beyond the five senses and allow their true colors of divinity to shine through!

We are all part of the Divine Source, and as such, we all possess the ability to develop beyond our human senses and to experience life in an amazing new vision, far beyond what the physical eyes can see. I hope that this little book has inspired you to tap into your Intuitive energies and that you discover how amazing you truly are!

I wish you nothing but joy and grace as you begin to harness your empathic energies and begin to blossom into a luminous vessel in order to assist others in their life journey. It has been a real pleasure to share my experiences and insight with you. Stay full of light and of love.

75

About the Author

Blanca is an internationally known author of 9 self-help books. She successfully maintained a private Holistic practice for over 15 years. As a Guru, she has attuned for 200 students to the art of Reiki across the globe and has countless of beloved devotes to her work and her expression of unconditional love.

She is currently touring on the East Coast, promoting her latest book release, "Female Divine, Hurt No More." Blanca regularly offers free 1-card readings on Facebook and also presents videos that offer the Oracle card of the day.

In addition to writing and her empathic work, Blanca is also a gifted healer and medium. To learn more about her work, visit her website at: http://blancabeyar.info or you can find her on Facebook.

Readers, if you found this book helpful, share your thoughts and comments! Visit Blanca on Facebook and share your comments. When you do, Blanca will offer you a personalized 3-card reading! Visit her page at:

https://www.facebook.com/blanca.greenberg

CPSIA information can be obtained
at www.ICGtesting.com
Printed in the USA
BVOW06s0518090317

478190BV00008B/95/P